BY MARIA WATKINS

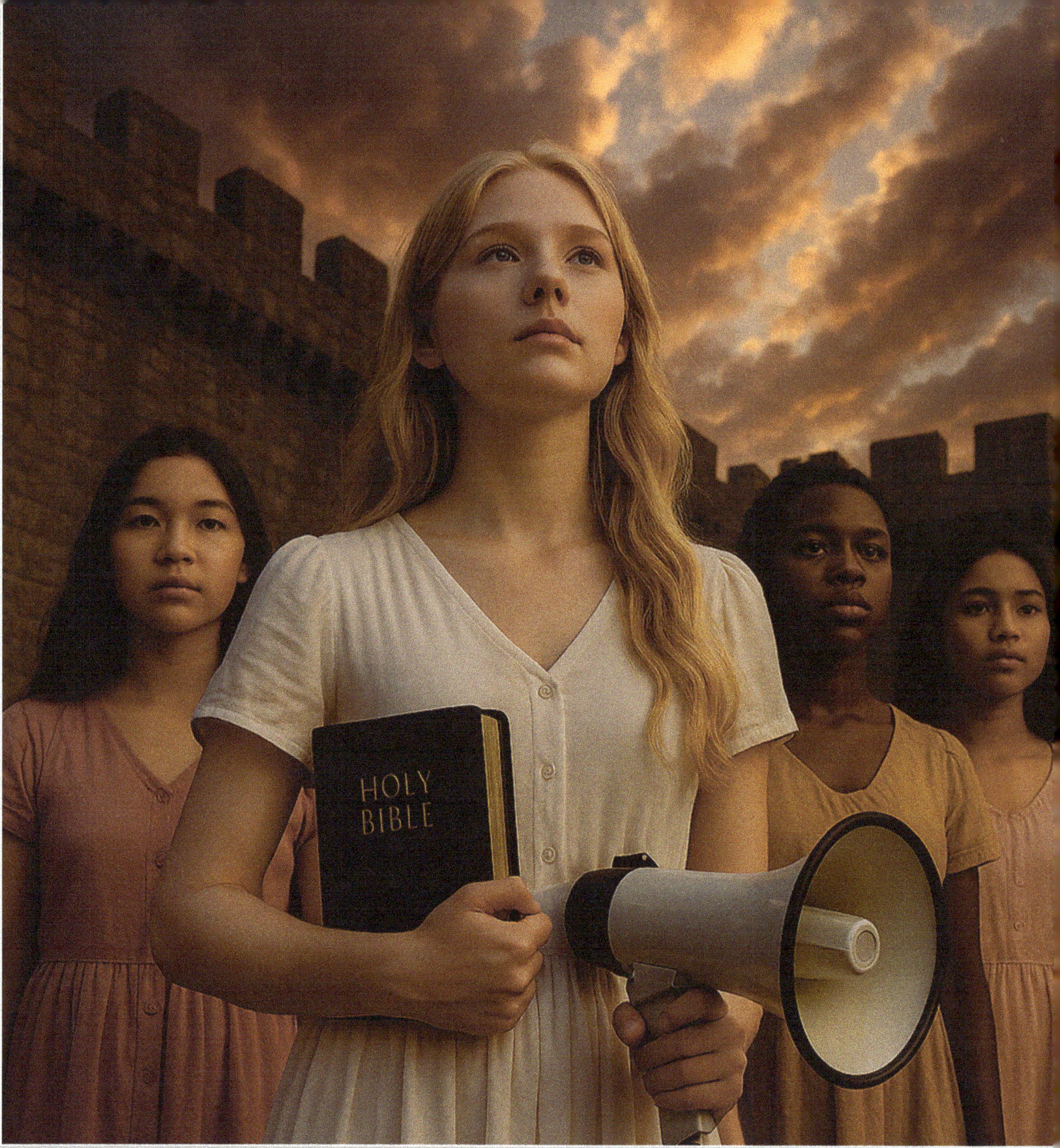

FIRST EDITION

A Discipleship Series by Empowered Legacy Ministries,
in partnership with Charity Heart Ministries.

THE RISING
JEWEL

THIS WORKBOOK BELONGS TO

_____

_____

_____

Author: Maria Watkins
Editor/Illustrator: Design: Olaiya Tolufashe
Cover Design: DoubleCi Studios

ISBN: 979-8-9997907-2-9

Scripture Acknowledgment:
All Scripture quotations, unless otherwise indicated, are taken from the New King James Version® (NKJV), © 1982 by Thomas Nelson. Used by permission.
All rights reserved.

All images and illustrations in this workbook were custom-designed and digitally created to support the themes and teachings shared within.

Publisher: Empowered Legacy Ministries, LLC

ALL ABOUT ME

Four words that describe me:

1 _____
2 _____
3 _____
4 _____

My name is: _____

I am _____ years old:

My birthday is on: _____

Im in the _____ grade

3   4 Words; 1 Me

1   Personal Info.

Food: _____

Color: _____

Subject: _____

Activity: _____

Animal: _____

Season: _____

Scripture: _____

I live in (city): _____

My school is: _____

My Best Friend is: _____

My family members are: _____
_____

2   People&Places

4   My Favourites

Dedication

To my beautiful nieces,
Daughters of the King
Created with beauty
Called with power

With every breath,
I carry you in this prayer:
May God use your life powerfully,
May you rise as the ones God created you to be.

Forever loved,
Forever cherished,
Forever valued,

This Book is for YOU.

With all my love,

Tia Mari

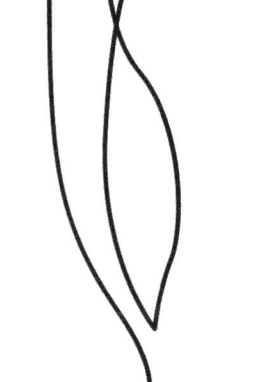

What to Expect
From the Study

01

Meet *Powerful* Women of Faith

You'll learn about the lives of six incredible women from the Word. Their lives might seem like a long time ago, but their struggles and triumphs are very much like yours today.

Learn About Your *Identity* in *Christ*

Each lesson, you will be discovering new truths about identity, courage, purity and purpose. You will see how much God loves you and why you are important to him and His plan right now, not later.

02

03

Get Closer to *God*; One step at a time.

You are going to journal, pray, affirm, and challenge yourself and talk to God honestly and hear what He says to your heart. You will have the chance to rise into the woman He created you to be.

From Girls to Jewels.
Time to *Step up!*

Hey Princess!

I'm so glad you're here — like really glad!

Just so you know, this study was designed exclusively for you. It's completely normal if you feel nervous or curious about what to expect in this life-changing Workbook, but you see, God is not anxious or unsure about you.

He already knows exactly what you need, and He brought you here as one of His precious Jewels on purpose. He sees your heart. He understands your questions. He knows your dreams, and He even hears your secret prayers.

Nothing in your life is hidden from Him.

Now, over the next six weeks, you will hear from God. You will also hear amazing stories about six women in the Bible. Women who were brave, honest, and full of faith.

Were they perfect? No, certainly not!

But God still used them in powerful ways. Before the six weeks are over, you will begin to see how God wants to use you for His glory, too.

Here is the truth: You were created on purpose, for a purpose. There is greatness inside of you that is waiting to rise. No mistake, no fear, no insecurity can cancel what God has placed within you.

So, open your heart wide. Allow God to speak. Allow Him to remind you of who you really are. You are not walking this alone; He is with you in every page, every prayer, every step.

You are at the beginning of your glorious story, and it is already beautiful.

Cheering you on:

Maria Watkins

connect@empoweredlegacyministries.com

empoweredlegacyministries.com

 Your **Checklist**

Your Bible (NKJV is great!)

This is your Sword! You'll be using it a lot; look for one with cool extras like maps and notes.

A Notebook or Journal

Write down what God shows you. These notes are treasures for your journey!

Fun Pens or Colors

Highlight verses that speak to you. Make it bold, make it yours.

This Workbook

This is your training manual. Keep it close and use it every week.

Worship Music Playlist

Music helps your heart get ready. Make or find a playlist that brings peace and power.

A Friend or Mentor

You don't have to do this alone! Grab a sister, bestie, or mentor to rise with you.

A Quiet Spot + Time

Choose a calm place and a regular time. This helps you stay focused and grow strong!

Your Study
Guide

Week 1: Esther

Chosen with Purpose: Discover how an ordinary girl stepped into extraordinary courage.

15

Week 2: Mary

A 'Yes' That Changed the World: See how Mary's simple "yes" to God made history.

31

Week 3: Deborah

Leading with Authority: Learn how Deborah led with wisdom and strength when the world around her was full of chaos.

47

Week 4: Ruth

Loyalty Leads to Legacy: Follow Ruth's journey of faithfulness. Her loyalty opened the door for God to use her life in His bigger story.

63

Week 5: Hannah

A Heart That Prays: Check out how Hannah poured out her heart to God and found strength in prayer.

79

Week 6: Sarah

Holding On When Hope Feels Distant: Walk with Sarah through seasons of waiting and doubt.

95

"

Here is the truth: You were created on
purpose, for a purpose. There is
greatness inside of you that
is waiting to rise.

Maria Watkins

15

ESTHER:

Chosen with Purpose

THEME
Identity & Courage

HERO
Esther

MAIN SCRIPTURE
Esther 2-4

Memory Verse

And who knows
but that you
have come to
your royal
position for
such a time
as this?

Esther 4:14

Lord, sometimes I wonder who I really am, but I know You made me for a reason. Help me stop comparing myself to others and see myself the way You see me.

Memory Verse Prayer

What We're Learning This Week:

We're learning that your worth and purpose don't come from what others think, but from who God says you are. Like Esther, you've been placed right where you are on purpose, and courage will unlock that calling. God can use your bravery and obedience to make a huge difference... just as He used Esther's.

Esther's *Story!*

Esther was not born famous, wealthy, or powerful. She was just an ordinary teen girl adopted by her cousin Mordecai when her parents passed away. She knew what it felt to go unnoticed, being different, and being on the outside.

But here's the amazing part: God saw her anyway. He chose her when she didn't feel, especially, special. Esther wasn't desperate for attention. She had humble strength, humility, and grace, and God's blessing followed her.

When she was made queen, her story didn't stop; it started. When her people (the children of Israel) were in danger, Esther was faced with a hard choice: remain silent and remain safe, or risk everything to do what is right. With faith that was not afraid, she said: "If I perish, I perish."

That's real courage, girls. Fear didn't disappear, her faith was only stronger. Her bold choice saved an entire nation.

Esther's life teaches us:

· You don't need a title or a crown to be chosen.

· You are already chosen by the King of Kings.

· Courage isn't about being fearless; it's about trusting God even when you're afraid.

And it's so true... You're not "just a girl." You are a Rising Jewel. You're a daughter of the King. You're chosen for such a time as this.

Learning

With Esther

01 **Esther was chosen even when she felt ordinary**

Even though Esther didn't come from royalty or status, **God saw her heart** and chose her to lead when others would **have overlooked her.**

i. Esther was a young _____ girl being raised by her cousin _____. **(Esther 2:7)**

ii. God gave her favor in the sight of everyone who _____ her. **(Esther 2:15)**

02 **Identity is not based on appearance or popularity**

Esther **didn't seek attention** or try to stand out, yet God honored **her humility** and chose her because of her heart, not her outward beauty.

iii. The King loved Esther more than all the other _____. **(Esther 2:17)**

iv. Esther was crowned _____ not because of looks, but because of God's hand on her life.

03 **Courage means doing the right thing even when it's scary**

Esther stepped **forward in faith**, risking everything to save her people, showing that real courage comes from trusting God even when you're afraid.

v. "If I _____, I _____." **(Esther 2:7)**

vi. Esther asked her people to _____ with her before going to the King. **(Esther 2:15)**

04 **Your purpose is bigger than just you**

Esther's **obedience** didn't just change her own life; it saved an entire nation, reminding us that God places us in positions of **influence to impact others.**

vii. "You have come to your royal position for such a _____ as this." **(Esther 2:7)**

viii. Your _____ opens the door for others to be free.

Let's Talk
About it

01.   What about Esther's story inspires you most?

02.   Ever laughed at something 'cause it felt impossible?

03.   What's one thing you'd try if fear wasn't in the way?

04.   Have you ever felt unqualified or overlooked? How does Esther's story encourage you?

Your Identity Pact

This week, write your own Identity Pact, then sign it as a promise between you and God:

"God, I believe You made me on purpose. I'm not a mistake or a background character. I choose to walk in who You say I am. I am chosen, loved, and brave. Use my life to help others, and give me courage to say yes to You."

Write yours:

_____

_____

_____

_____

_____

Keep this in your Bible or journal to remind yourself: You're chosen. Always.

_____
Signed

_____
Date

Dig Deeper

God wants to talk to YOU—not just your group or leader! This section is your quiet time with Him. What to Do:

01. Look up each verse in your Bible (take your time).

02. Write the verse in your own words.

03. Ask: "What is God trying to tell ME?"

04. Write it down below!

01. Psalm 139:13–14

Write the verse here:

_____

_____

_____

What does it mean to you?

_____

_____

_____

_____

02. Jeremiah 1:5

Write the verse here:

_____

_____

_____

What does it mean to you?

_____

_____

_____

_____

03. 1 Peter 2:9

Write the verse here:

What does it mean to you?

04. Isaiah 41:10

Write the verse here:

What does it mean to you?

LET'S PRAY

Dear God,

Thank You for Esther's story. She was young, ordinary, and scared, but You still chose her. Remind me that I'm chosen too. Even when I feel small or not enough, show me You have a plan for my life. Give me boldness to stand up, courage to speak truth, and faith to trust You all the way. In Jesus' name, amen.

Time to Take Action

Be Brave Like Esther: Your choices shape your future. Decide what to stand up for, drop, keep holding on to, and grow deeper in.

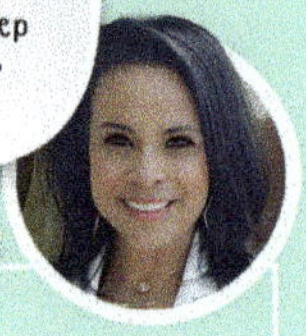

Stop Doing	Answer:
Do Less	Answer:
Keep Doing	Answer:
Do More	Answer:
Start Doing	Answer:

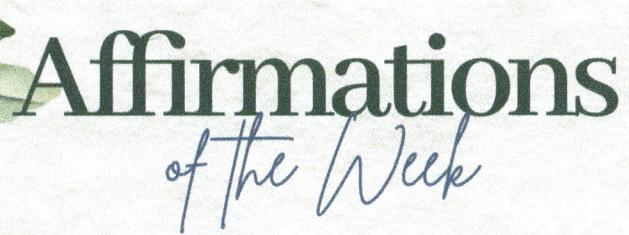

Affirmations
of the Week

01

I am chosen, loved, and brave. I belong to God. I walk in His strength

02

I'm a Precious Jewel. I'm bold like Esther. I'm loved by the King of Kings.

03

My identity is not in what people say; My Identity is in Jesus, the risen Christ.

04

I live by faith. I walk in courage. I'm not a slave to fear.

05

I'm not just a girl. I am a daughter of the King, called to shine in dark places.

06

I'm not invisible. I am seen. I'm beloved I'm set apart for such a time as this.

These are your Power-Words. Speak these over yourself every day this week!

SCAN ME

From God's Heart to *Yours!*

This page is just for you and God.

Take a breath. Slow down. Let the noise fade. God has been speaking all week, not only through the story of Esther, but also in those little moments when something clicked, or a verse felt like it was written just for you.

Now it's your turn to talk back. Don't worry about fancy words. God doesn't need that. He just wants the real you. Be honest. Be raw. Be open. Write down what stood out, what you felt, or what you think God is nudging you to do next. This is where growth happens... when your heart connects with His.

What do you feel like God is saying to you this week? Journal your thoughts below.

My Notes from God this Week:

notes

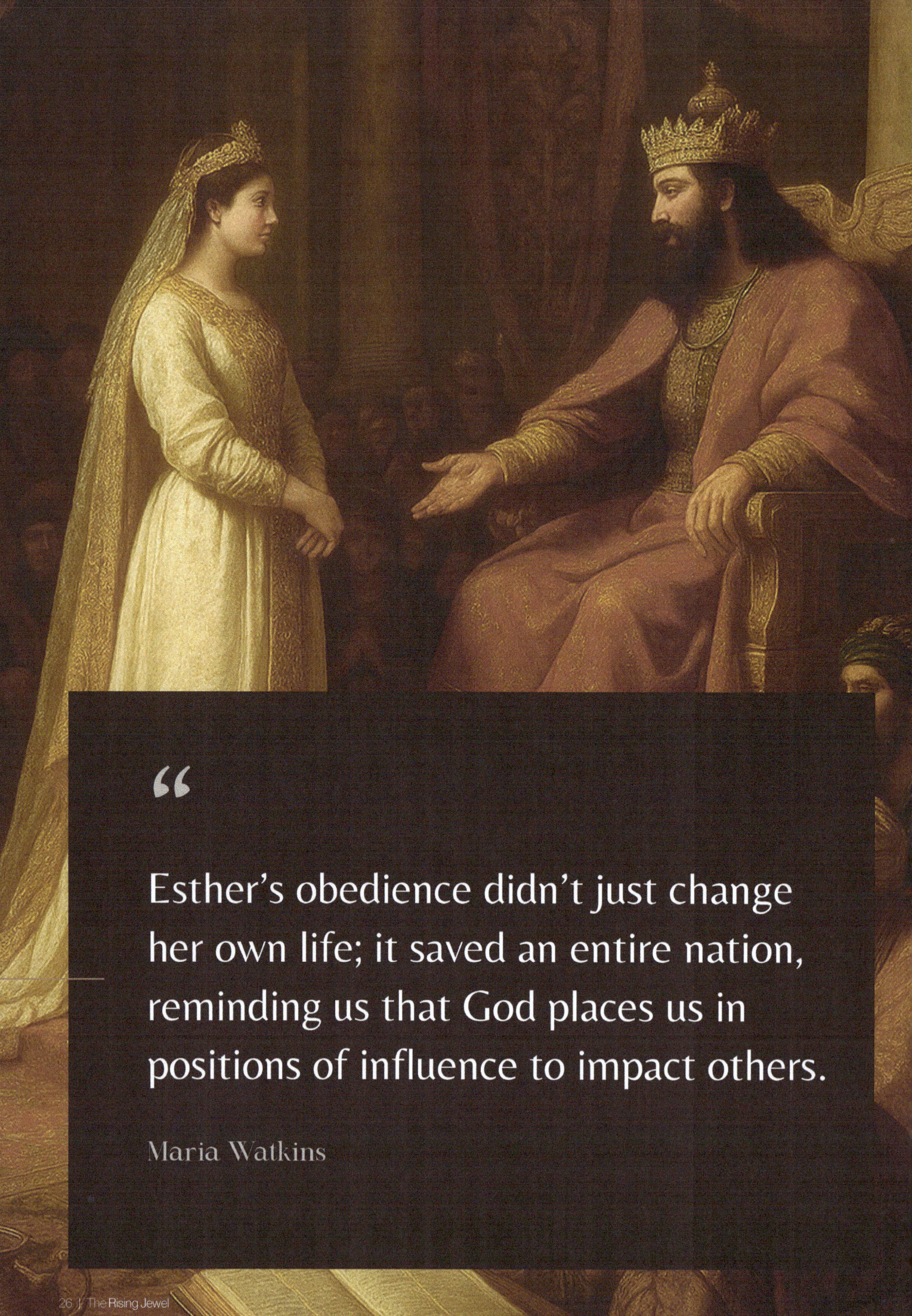

"

Esther's obedience didn't just change her own life; it saved an entire nation, reminding us that God places us in positions of influence to impact others.

Maria Watkins

Help Esther find her crown!

Game Time

Homework

		Yes	No
01	Esther was chosen as queen of England.		
02	The King reminded Esther she was in the palace "for such a time as this."		
03	Esther fasted and prayed before going to the king.		
04	Going to the king without being called was completely safe.		
05	Esther risked her life to save her people.		
06	God can use young people like Esther to change history.		

WEEK TWO

WEEK TWO

MARY:

A 'Yes' That Changed the World

One simple, faith-filled "yes"

Theme	Hero	Main Scriptures
Purity & Obedience	**Mary**	**Luke 1:26–38**

Memory Verse

Blessed is she who has believed that the Lord would fulfill his promises to her!

Luke 1:45

> Lord, help me believe You fully, even when I can't see the whole picture. Give me Mary's quiet strength, and let my 'yes' echo for Your glory.
>
> *Memory Verse Prayer*

What We're Learning This Week:

Mary shows us that purity and obedience go hand in hand. A pure heart trusts God even when the road feels confusing. One simple, faith-filled "yes" can open the door for God to do something huge through your life.

Mary's Heart: Pure, Brave, and *Chosen!*

Mary wasn't famous, she wasn't wealthy... she was just a normal teenage girl in Nazareth, a small village in Israel. No platform. No spotlight. A life quietly set apart for God. What made Mary shine wasn't her looks or her talents; it was her heart. She lived pure. She lived surrendered. That's what God noticed.

Then, everything changed. An angel showed up and called her "highly favored." God had a plan that would flip her whole life upside down: she would carry Jesus, the Son of God. People wouldn't understand. Rumors would spread. Her future plans would look completely different. But Mary said yes anyway.

Her yes wasn't small. It was a yes to purity under pressure. A yes to obey when it didn't all make sense. A yes to God's plan over people's opinions. That's courage.

Mary's story proves this: purity is strength, obedience is power, and your yes can change the world. God still chooses girls who are willing to walk in purity. You are one of them.

Learning

01 **Mary was young, but her heart was ready.**

Mary's age **didn't limit her purpose** because God saw a heart that was fully available to Him and ready to carry something holy.

i. Mary lived in the town of _____, a small and ordinary place. **(Luke 1:26)**

ii. The angel called her "highly _____." **(Luke 1:28)**

02 **Purity begins with the heart.**

Mary lived a life that honored God, showing us that purity is more than just physical choices; it is **a heart set apart for Him.**

iii. The angel told Mary she had found _____ with God. **(Luke 1:30)**

iv. Purity is not just about actions, it's about _____ God above all.

03 **Obedience often comes before understanding.**

Even when Mary **couldn't see** how everything would unfold, **she still trusted God** and said yes to His will with faith and humility.

v. Mary asked, "How can this be?" but still said, "Let it be to me according to your _____." **(Luke 1:38)**

vi. Faith is choosing to _____ even when you don't fully understand.

04 **God uses simple yeses to do extraordinary things.**

Mary's **quiet surrender** made room for Jesus to enter the world, proving that small, obedient steps can lead to **world-changing** outcomes.

vii. Mary's obedience brought _____ into the world.

viii. Your obedience brings God's _____ into your world.

Let's Talk
About it

01.   What do you think gave Mary the courage to say yes to God?

02.   What do you think purity looks like in your heart, not just your actions?

03.   How can obedience become an act of worship?

04.   What do you think purity looks like in your heart, not just your actions?

Your 'Yes' Commitment

Write your own "yes" to God this week. It doesn't need to be fancy; just real. Example:

"God, even when I don't fully get it, I choose to trust You. I want to live pure and stay ready to say yes to Your plan. My life belongs to You. Let it be to me as You say."

Write yours:

_____

_____

_____

_____

_____

_____

Put it somewhere you'll see it this week and whisper your yes every time.

_____
Signed

_____
Date

Dig Deeper

it's time to slow down and really listen to what God says about you. Ready? Grab your Bible, a pen, and some quiet time. What to Do:

01. Look up each verse in your Bible (take your time).

02. Write the verse in your own words.

03. Ask: "What is God trying to tell ME?"

04. Write it down below!

01. Luke 1:38

Write the verse here:

What does it mean to you?

02. Psalm 24:3–4

Write the verse here:

What does it mean to you?

03. John 14:15

Write the verse here:

_____

_____

_____

What does it mean to you?

_____

_____

_____

_____

04. Proverbs 3:5–6

Write the verse here:

_____

_____

_____

What does it mean to you?

_____

_____

_____

_____

LET'S PRAY

Father,

Thank You for Mary's example of purity and obedience. You didn't choose her because she was flawless, but because her heart was ready to trust You. Teach me to have that same kind of trust. When life feels confusing or scary, remind me that You are right here with me. Give me the courage to say "yes" to You, even when it's tough. My heart is Yours. Use my life to shine for You. In Jesus' name. Amen.

Time to Take Action

Stop Doing

Answer:

Do Less

Answer:

Keep Doing

Answer:

Do More

Answer:

Start Doing

Answer:

Affirmations
of the Week

01

I'm not lucky, I am blessed and highly favored by God.

02

I'm not weak. My purity is my strength, my shield, and my crown.

03

I'm not ordinary. My "yes" to God carries the power to change the world.

04

I'm not afraid. I am brave. I trust God's plan. Even when I can't see it.

05

I'm not ordinary. I am a daughter of the King, set apart for His unstoppable purpose.

06

I'm not chasing likes. I already walk in the approval of God, my Father.

Say them out loud. Believe every word. This is who you are. Speak these every day this week!

SCAN ME

From God's Heart to *Yours!*

This page is just for you and God.

God has been whispering to your heart all week; through the Bible, your thoughts, you quiet moments of prayer. Maybe it was a verse that stuck with you, a new way you saw His love, or a gentle nudge you felt inside when you were still.

Here's your chance to write it down. God is not looking for you to impress Him. He wants your honesty.Let it be your heart-to-Heart time with Him. The Holy Spirit is ready to meet you right here.

Use this space to share your real thoughts, your questions, and even your struggles.

My Notes from God this Week:

notes

"

When life feels confusing or scary, remind me that You are right here with me. Give me the courage to say "yes" to You, even when it's tough. My heart is Yours. Use my life to shine for You.

Maria Watkins

HELP MARY REACH THE CRADLE!

YES TO GOD'S PLAN

NAZARETH

Game Time

Homework

01

An angel appear to Mary to announce she would be the mother of Jesus

Yes No

02

The angel called Mary "highly intelligent"

Yes No

03

Mary was young, and her heart wasn't ready

Yes No

04

Mary said "Let it be to me according to your mercy."

Yes No

05

Mary's story teaches us that God can use anyone, even a teenager, to do His will.

Yes No

06

Mary's obedience brought Joseph into the world.

Yes No

DEBORAH:

Leading with Authority

Called to Lead!

THEME
Authority

HERO
Deborah

MAIN SCRIPTURE
Judges 4:1–16

Memory Verse

Behold, I give you the authority to trample on serpents and scorpions, and over all the power of the enemy, and nothing shall by any means hurt you.

Luke 10:19

Dear Jesus, help me to lead with humility, boldness, and a pure heart. Teach me to listen first, speak life, and to use my authority to show Your love.

Memory Verse Prayer

What We're Learning This Week:

This week we're learning that authority doesn't come from being popular, having a title, or being the loudest voice in the room. Real authority comes from a heart that is pure, obedient, and surrendered to God. Like Deborah, you carry more influence than you realize, and God wants to show you how to use it with courage and wisdom.

Let's talk about Deborah!

Deborah lived in a time when Israel was in chaos. People were afraid. Leaders were silent. Hope was fading. The noise of fear and despair filled the land, drowning out courage and hope.

But Deborah didn't let the noise around her drown out God's voice inside her. She sat still with God, and that stillness gave her courage. She led when others backed down. She spoke with confidence because she first listened in prayer.

Deborah was a judge, a prophetess, and even called a "mother of Israel." But her authority didn't come from her title. It came from her closeness to God. Her leadership flowed out of purity... purity in her worship, purity in her motives, purity in her purpose.

When God gave the word of victory, she didn't hesitate. She called Barak, the military leader, to action. When he hesitated, Deborah stood firm. She stepped into a role many thought wasn't for women, yet her boldness was fueled by obedience, not pride.

Deborah shows us that true authority doesn't mean controlling others. It means being connected to God's presence, hearing His voice, and having the courage to obey.

And here's the truth: you may not feel like a leader yet, but if God's Spirit is in you, your voice matters. Like Deborah, you can bring courage, hope, and victory to the people around you.

"

**Deborah didn't let the noise around her drown out God's voice inside her...
She spoke with confidence because she first listened in prayer**

Maria Watkins

Learning

With Deborah

01 **Deborah's leadership came from her relationship with God.**

Deborah **led with confidence** because she first listened to God in stillness and allowed His presence to shape her wisdom and voice.

i. Deborah was a prophetess and _____ of Israel. **(Judges 4:4)**

ii. She sat under the palm tree of _____. **(Judges 4:5)**

02 **Spiritual authority starts with purity of heart.**

Deborah's influence was powerful because **her heart was clean before God,** and her motives were anchored in honoring Him.

iii. Deborah judged Israel because she listened to _____. **(Judges 4:4–5)**

iv. Purity gives _____ to hear God's instructions clearly. **(Matthew 5:8)**

03 **Authority is strengthened by obedience.**

Deborah didn't wait for **approval from others;** her strength came from her **willingness to act** when God gave direction.

v. Deborah told Barak, "Has not the Lord God of Israel _____ you?" **(Judges 4:6)**

vi. She walked in _____ before walking in leadership.

04 **God uses your voice to bring victory.**

Deborah's obedience and courage became the turning point for a nation, showing us that **our voices can release freedom** when we speak what God says.

vii. Deborah said, "I will surely _____ with you." **(Judges 4:9)**

viii. The battle was won because _____ obeyed God's voice.

Let's Talk
About it

01.   What do you admire most about Deborah's leadership?

02.   How can you grow in listening to God like Deborah did?

03.   How can you grow in listening to God like Deborah did?

04.   Have you ever felt like your voice didn't matter? What would change if you believed God gave you influence?

Your Leadership Prayer

Write a short leadership prayer to God. Ask Him to give you a clean heart and bold obedience like Deborah:

"God, I want to be a girl who listens for Your voice. I don't want to speak unless You've spoken first. Make my heart pure, my spirit bold, and my voice strong with Your truth. Use me to bring courage and wisdom to others. I trust You to lead me."

Write yours:

_____

_____

_____

_____

_____

Place this in a space where you can see it this week and pray over it daily.

_____

Signed

_____

Date

Time to block out the noise and focus. God has truth to speak. Are you ready to hear it? Get your Bible and a Pen. Let's do this.

01. Look up each verse in your Bible (take your time).

02. Write the verse in your own words.

03. Ask: "What is God trying to tell ME?"

04. Write it down below!

01. Psalm 24:3–4

Write the verse here:

_____

_____

_____

What does it mean to you?

_____

_____

_____

02. Isaiah 30:15

Write the verse here:

_____

_____

_____

What does it mean to you?

_____

_____

_____

03. Proverbs 31:25–26

Write the verse here:

_____
_____
_____

What does it mean to you?

_____
_____
_____
_____

04. James 3:17

Write the verse here:

_____
_____
_____

What does it mean to you?

_____
_____
_____
_____

LET'S PRAY

Father,

Thank You for the example of Deborah. She didn't quit when things got tough. She listened to You and obeyed with boldness. Show me how to lead with a clean heart. Remind me that my strength is in Your presence, not trying to impress men. Give me boldness that is Yours, and let my voice speak out for Your glory. In Jesus' name, amen.

Time To Take Action

Stop Doing

Answer:

Do Less

Answer:

Keep Doing

Answer:

Do More

Answer:

Start Doing

Answer:

Affirmations
of the Week

01

I'm not just another voice. I listen first, then I speak with wisdom.

02

I'm not just walking. I lead with faith, I speak with courage, I walk in victory!

03

I'm not just talking. My heart is pure. My words bring life.

04

I'm not just speaking. God's voice is my guide, obedience is my power.

05

I'm not just a girl. I'm a Jewel. A daughter of the King of Kings. I carry His authority.

06

I'm not average. I carry a pure heart, a sound mind, and the unstoppable Spirit of God.

Say these out loud. Believe them. This is your true identity. Speak them every day this week!

SCAN ME

From God's Heart to *Yours!*
This page is just for you and God.

Deborah lived in a time of confusion, but her heart was steady. She stayed close to God, and it gave her clarity and courage. This week, God may have spoken to your heart in a way that felt personal. Take time to reflect on those moments.

Write down what you sensed God saying, what Scripture touched your heart, or any thoughts that keep coming back to you. This is not just journaling. This is communion. This is you receiving from the One who made you.

What do you feel like God is saying to you this week? Journal your thoughts below.

My Notes from God this Week:

notes

> "
>
> Deborah was a judge, a prophetess, and even called a "mother of Israel." But her authority didn't come from her title. It came from her closeness to God.
>
> Maria Watkins

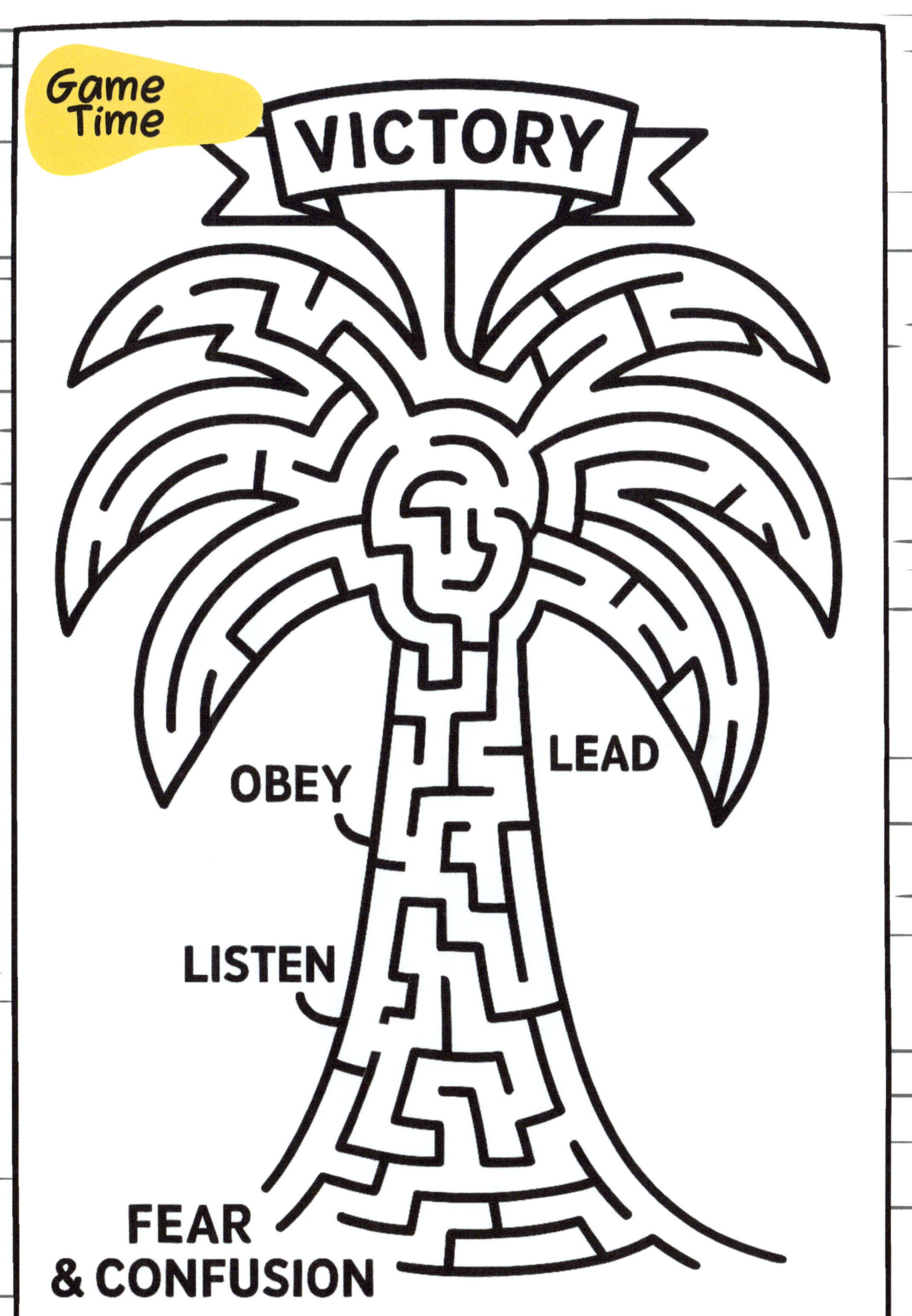

Homework

		Yes	No
01	Deborah was a prophetess and a judge in Israel.	☐	☐
02	Deborah sat under an apple tree to give wisdom and judgment.	☐	☐
03	Deborah rose with fear when others held back.	☐	☐
04	Deborah's influence was powerful because her heart was clean before God.	☐	☐
05	Deborah command Barak to gather 100,000 men.	☐	☐
06	Deborah's story teaches us that God uses our voice to bring victory	☐	☐

63.

RUTH:
Loyalty Leads to Legacy

Loyalty & Legacy

Theme	Hero	Main Scripture
Calling & Destiny	**Ruth**	**Ruth 1-2**

Memory Verse

The Lord repay your work, and a full reward be given you by the Lord God of Israel, under whose wings you have come for refuge.

Ruth 2:12

> God, like Ruth, I come under Your wings for safety and covering. I give You my fears and trust You to guide every step. Help me stay faithful even when no one notices.
>
> *Memory Verse Prayer*

What We're Learning This Week:

Ruth shows us that calling doesn't always come with a spotlight or stage. Sometimes it's found in small choices, like being loyal, faithful, and pure in heart. Your past or your background doesn't cancel out your future. When you stay close to God and walk with integrity, He leads you step by step into your destiny.

Your Loyalty Can Lead to Your Destiny... Just Like *Ruth!*

Ruth didn't have it easy. She was a widow, a foreigner, and a young woman in a culture that didn't value her much. She lost her husband, her plans, and her sense of security. Life could have crushed her, but Ruth didn't give up.

Instead, she chose loyalty. She stayed with her mother-in-law, Naomi, and more importantly, she stayed with God. When Ruth said, "Your people will be my people, and your God, my God," she wasn't just promising to Naomi; she was stepping into a brand-new identity and surrendering her future to God.

Ruth's beauty wasn't about looks. It was her heart. She was hardworking, humble, and faithful even when no one was watching. That quiet strength caught the attention of Boaz, a godly man who saw her character first.

Her story proves that destiny often begins in ordinary places. Ruth wasn't chasing fame or recognition; she was just doing the right thing in the fields, one day at a time, and God turned her small, hidden acts of loyalty into a legacy that reached all the way to Jesus.

So, if you've ever felt overlooked, unqualified, or like your life is too small to matter, remember Ruth. God sees your loyalty. He sees your faithfulness. Nothing is wasted when your heart is surrendered to Him.

01

Ruth chose loyalty when it cost her everything.

Ruth stayed with Naomi when she could have left, proving that **faithfulness in small decisions** opens doors to greater purpose.

i. Ruth said, "Where you go, I will _____." **(Ruth 1:16)**

ii. She left her country and her _____ to follow God.

02

Purity of motive brings favor.

Ruth **wasn't trying to impress anyone**, she simply walked with integrity, and her character spoke louder than any title.

iii. Boaz told Ruth he had heard about her _____ and kindness to Naomi. **(Ruth 2:11)**

iv. Ruth found _____ in the eyes of Boaz because of her heart.

03

Destiny often begins in ordinary places.

Ruth found her future in a field, reminding us that **simple obedience** can lead to supernatural outcomes.

v. Ruth worked in the _____ to provide for Naomi and herself. **(Ruth 2:3)**

vi. Her steps were ordered by _____, even when she didn't see it.

04

Legacy is built through small acts of faith.

Ruth's decision to **honor God** and **stay faithful** made her part of Jesus' family line, proving that God uses loyalty to build legacy.

vii. Ruth became the great-grandmother of _____. **(Ruth 4:17)**

viii. God brought _____ through her obedience.

Let's Talk
About it

01.   What part of Ruth's story do you connect with the most?

02.   Have you ever made a hard choice out of loyalty or faithfulness?

03.   How does Ruth's story encourage you about your own future?

04.   What does it mean to have purity of heart in the ordinary things?

Your Leadership Prayer

Take a moment to write your own prayer about being loyal and faithful. Tell God you trust Him with your next steps. Example:

"God, I want to be like Ruth: faithful, loyal, and full of quiet courage. When things feel small or hard, keep me close to You. I choose integrity, I choose trust, and I choose You. Build a legacy through my obedience."

Write yours:

_____

_____

_____

_____

_____

Keep this where you'll see it, and pray it on the days you feel discouraged or overlooked.

_____
Signed

_____
Date

Dig Deeper

Pause for a sec. Time to hear what God says about you. Grab your Bible, a pen, and find a quiet spot. Ready? Let's go.

01. Look up each verse in your Bible (take your time).

02. Write the verse in your own words.

03. Ask: "What is God trying to tell ME?"

04. Write it down below!

01. Ruth 1:16–17

Write the verse here:

What does it mean to you?

02. Galatians 6:9

Write the verse here:

What does it mean to you?

03. Matthew 25:21

Write the verse here:

_____
_____
_____

What does it mean to you?

_____
_____
_____
_____

04. Psalm 37:5

Write the verse here:

_____
_____
_____

What does it mean to you?

_____
_____
_____

LET'S PRAY

Dear God,

Thank You for Ruth's story. Her loyalty and pure heart remind me that I don't need to chase attention or prove myself. I just need to walk with You. Teach me to trust You in every season, even in the small, ordinary days. Give me a heart like Ruth's; steady, kind, and full of faith. Take my quiet "yes" and use it for something that lasts. In Jesus' name, amen.

Time To Take Action

Stop Doing

Answer:

Do Less

Answer:

Keep Doing

Answer:

Do More

Answer:

Start Doing

Answer:

Affirmations
of the Week

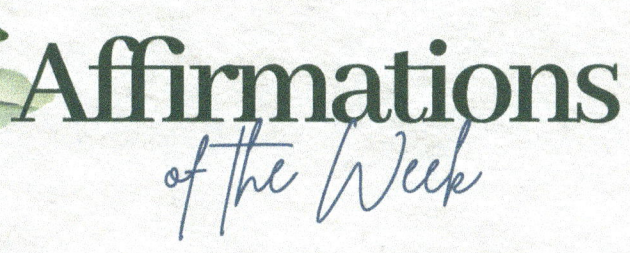

01

I'm not just surviving. I am Loyal. I am faithful to God, even when it's hard.

02

I'm not ignored. I'm not overlooked. God sees my loyalty, and rewards my heart.

03

I'm not ordinary. I am amazing. I am a daughter with destiny.

04

I'm not giving up. I'm walking with integrity. Every step moves me closer to purpose.

05

I'm not wasting time. I'm trusting God with my future. My loyalty is building a legacy.

06

I'm not chasing recognition. I'm chasing purpose. God is leading me into destiny

Say them out loud. Believe every word. This is who you are. Speak these every day this week!

SCAN ME

From God's Heart to *Yours!*

This page is just for you and God.

This week, you learned how Ruth's loyalty and quiet faithfulness shaped her destiny. She didn't wait for life to get easier or for everything to make sense; she stayed faithful right where she was. God met her in the ordinary, turning her small "yes" into a legacy.

Has God spoken to you this week? Did He remind you that He is present in those hidden places? That He sees your loyalty, your love, and your faithfulness? Was there a verse, a thought, or a moment that hit your heart?

No matter what it is, put it here. This is how you learn — from His heart to yours.

My Notes from God this Week:

notes

> "
> Ruth wasn't chasing fame or recognition; she was just doing the right thing in the fields, one day at a time, and God turned her small, hidden acts of loyalty into a legacy that reached all the way to Jesus.

Maria Watkins

HELP RUTH FIND HER WAY TO BETHLEHEM

BETHLEHEM

FAITHFULNESS

OBEDIENCE

MOAB

Game Time

Homework

01 Ruth left Naomi behind and returned to her own family.

Yes ☐ No ☐

02 Ruth caught Boaz's attention because of her loyalty and character.

Yes ☐ No ☐

03 Ruth became the great-grandmother of King Saul.

Yes ☐ No ☐

04 Ruth reminds us that Destiny often begins in ordinary places.

Yes ☐ No ☐

05 Ruth's life shows us that God only uses people with perfect backgrounds.

Yes ☐ No ☐

06 Ruth was an Israelite that got married to a Boaz a Moabite

Yes ☐ No ☐

HANNAH:
Tears, Trust, and Triumph

WEEK FIVE

"Surrounded by people who had what she was praying for, she carried empty arms and a heavy heart."

"Your prayers matter!"

THEME
Identity & Faith

HERO
Hannah

MAIN SCRIPTURE
1 Samuel 1:1–20

Memory Verse

Be anxious for nothing, but in everything by prayer and supplication, with thanksgiving, let your requests be made known to God.

Philippians 4:6

God, teach me to be the kind of girl who prays first and stresses less. Shape me in the waiting. Build my faith in the quiet. I trust You with it all.

Memory Verse Prayer

What We're Learning This Week:

"This week, you'll learn that prayer isn't just asking God for things; it's trusting Him, surrendering to Him, and believing He is faithful even in your waiting. Hannah's story reminds us that your identity grows stronger every time you run to God. Even when life feels unfair or silent, your prayers still matter to Him.

Hannah's *Yes!*

Sometimes silence feels louder than words. That was Hannah's life. She longed for a child, but year after year, nothing changed. Surrounded by people who had what she was praying for, she carried empty arms and a heavy heart.

On top of that, she had someone in her life who made things worse; mocking her pain and cutting her down with cruel words. It would have been easy for Hannah to give up or grow bitter. But she didn't. Instead of running to people, she ran to God.

Her prayer wasn't fancy. She didn't try to impress anyone. Her lips moved but no sound came out. Tears streamed down her face. To others, it looked strange, but to God, it was beautiful. Her honesty was worship.

In that moment, something shifted inside her. Her situation didn't change immediately, but her heart did.She walked away with peace, not because she had the answer in her hands, but because she had put everything in God's hands.

Hannah's identity wasn't defined by her struggle. It was shaped by her surrender. Her pure, yielded heart became the place where purpose was born. When God gave her Samuel, she didn't cling tighter; she gave him back to the Lord. Her "yes" to God made space for a prophet to rise and for a nation to be impacted.

Her story reminds us: prayer isn't just about getting what we ask for. It's about stepping into God's bigger story: living out His will and being used to impact others.

Learning

01 ## Hannah brought her pain to God, not people.

Hannah didn't let her emotions **lead her away from God;** she allowed them to draw her closer to Him through prayer.

i. Hannah was deeply in _____ and prayed to the Lord. (1 Samuel 1:10)

ii. She poured out her soul before _____. (1 Samuel 1:15)

02 ## God values a pure and surrendered heart.

Hannah's prayers **were not selfish,** they were born out of **surrender and trust,** which moved the heart of God.

iii. She made a _____, offering her son back to the Lord. (1 Samuel 1:11)

iv. God remembered her because her heart was _____ before Him.

03 ## Prayer changes your heart before it changes your situation.

Even before she saw the answer, Hannah received peace **by trusting** that God had heard her.

v. After praying, she went her way and her face was no longer _____. (1 Samuel 1:18)

vi. She believed that the Lord would _____ her request.

04 ## Your prayers are connected to your calling.

Hannah's **willingness to pray** and trust **brought Samuel into the world,** proving that prayer births purpose.

vii. The child born to Hannah was named _____. (1 Samuel 1:20)

viii. Samuel would later become a _____ in Israel, showing how Hannah's faith impacted generations. (1 Samuel 3:20)

Let's Talk
About it

01.　　What do you admire most about the way Hannah prayed?

02.　　Is there something you've been afraid to talk to God about?

03.　　What does it mean to trust God before you see results?

04.　　How can prayer help you walk in your true identity?

Your **Surrender Prayer**

This week, write a personal prayer to God. Be real. Share your hopes, your fears, and your dreams. Don't hold anything back.

God, I give You my heart. Even when I don't understand what You're doing, I choose to trust you. I bring my pain, my dreams, and my waiting to You. Teach me to walk in faith like Hannah. Let my life bring You glory.

Write yours:

_____

_____

_____

_____

_____

Keep this where you'll see it, and pray it on the days you feel discouraged or overlooked.

_____
Signed

_____
Date

Dig  Deeper

Pause for a sec. Time to hear what God says about you. Grab your Bible, a pen, and find a quiet spot. Ready? Let's go.

01. Look up each verse in your Bible (take your time).

02. Write the verse in your own words.

03. Ask: "What is God trying to tell ME?"

04. Write it down below!

01. 1 Samuel 1:10–11

Write the verse here:

_____

_____

_____

What does it mean to you?

_____

_____

_____

_____

02. Psalm 34:18

Write the verse here:

_____

_____

_____

What does it mean to you?

_____

_____

_____

_____

03. Philippians 4:6–7

Write the verse here:

What does it mean to you?

04. Romans 12:12

Write the verse here:

What does it mean to you?

Father,

Thank You for hearing me, even when my prayers come out as tears. Thank You for Hannah's story that reminds me I'm never alone and never forgotten. Teach me to pray with faith, not fear. Help me let go of what I can't control. Keep my heart pure and close to You. I believe You are faithful.

In Jesus' name, amen.

Time to Take Action

Stop Doing

Answer:

Do Less

Answer:

Keep Doing

Answer:

Do More

Answer:

Start Doing

Answer:

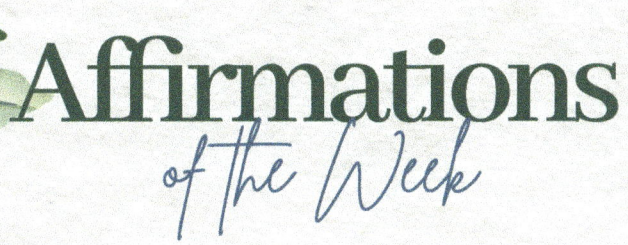

Affirmations
of the Week

01

I'm not just waiting. I'm surrendering in faith. I'm trusting God's timing.

02

I'm not defined by silence. I'm not empty. I am filled with peace.

03

I'm not small. I am a daughter of God. I birth destiny through prayer.

04

I'm not forgotten. I'm seen. I'm known. I'm heard by God.

05

I'm not powerless. My prayers carry weight, power, and purpose.

06

I'm not ruled by fear. I'm powered by faith.

Say these out loud every day this week. Speak them like you believe them, because they're true.

SCAN ME

From God's Heart to *Yours!*
This page is just for you and God.

This week you learned how Hannah poured out her heart in prayer. How she didn't let her pain push her away. She brought it honestly to God, and in that place of surrender, peace and purpose were born. Now it's your turn.

Did God stir something in your heart this week? Did He remind you that He hears even your quietest prayers? Did He show you that waiting isn't wasted, but shaping you?

Whatever it was, write it down. That's how you grow — from His heart... to yours.

My Notes from God this Week:

_____

_____

_____

_____

_____

_____

_____

notes

"

[Hannah's] story reminds us: prayer isn't just about getting what we ask for. It's about stepping into God's bigger story: living out His will and being used to impact others.

Maria Watkins

PROMISE

SURRENDER

FAITH

PRAYER

Game Time

Homework

01 Hannah poured out her heart before the Lord at the temple.

Yes ☐   No ☐

02 Eli thought Hannah was hungry when he saw her praying.

Yes ☐   No ☐

03 Hannah gave up on prayer when it felt too hard.

Yes ☐   No ☐

04 God remembered Hannah and answered her prayer.

Yes ☐   No ☐

05 Hannah "yes" to God made space for a prophet to rise and for a nation to be impacted.

Yes ☐   No ☐

06 From Hannah we learnt that Prayer changes your heart before it changes your situation.

Yes ☐   No ☐

SARAH

From Doubt to JOY

God's timing brings joy.

Theme	Hero	Main Scripture
God's Timing	**Sarah**	**Genesis 17–21**

Memory Verse

He did not waver at the promise of God through unbelief, but was strengthened in faith, giving glory to God.

Romans 4:20

> God, I don't want to waver in doubt. Strengthen my faith like Abraham and Sarah. Teach me to trust Your Word, even when nothing looks possible.
>
> *Memory Verse Prayer*

What We're Learning This Week:

This week, Sarah shows us that waiting doesn't mean God has forgotten. His promises don't expire. Even when faith feels fragile, He remains faithful. God's timing may not match ours, but it is always perfect; and it always brings joy.

Faith Through Silent *Years!*

Some promises take a long time to show up. That's where Sarah lived. God had promised her a child, a legacy. But year after year, nothing changed. She grew older. Hope grew dimmer. Disappointment weighed heavily. She had waited so long that laughter became her defense.

So when God said again she would have a son, she laughed, not because it was funny, but because it was too hard to believe. Could something that seemed impossible really happen after all this time?

Sarah's journey wasn't flawless. She tried to make the promise happen her own way by giving Hagar to Abraham. It only complicated things. But God didn't cancel His plan. He didn't take His promise back just because Sarah doubted.

And when Isaac was born, her laughter turned to joy. The same woman who once laughed in disbelief now laughed with delight, holding her miracle in her arms. God had kept His word, not on her timeline, but on His.

Sarah's story reminds us: waiting is never wasted. Even when faith feels small, God is still faithful. Even when the years feel long, He is still working. His promises don't expire, and His timing always brings joy.

01 — God's promises are often delayed, not denied.

Sarah waited many years **for the promise to be fulfilled,** showing that delay does not mean God has forgotten.

i. God told Abraham that Sarah would bear a _____.   (1 (Genesis 17:19)

ii. Though she was past the age of childbearing, she still received the _____. (Genesis 21:2)

02 — Faith can feel fragile, but God remains faithful.

Sarah laughed in disbelief, **yet God didn't reject her;** He gently confirmed His word with grace.

iii. Sarah said, "Shall I surely bear a child, since I am _____?"   (1 Samuel 1:11)

iv. The Lord asked, "Is anything too _____ for the Lord?"   (Genesis 18:14)

03 — God works even through our mistakes.

Though Sarah tried to take control by giving Hagar to Abraham, **God still redeemed the story.**

v. Sarah gave her maidservant _____ to Abraham.   (Genesis 16:3)

vi. Even when we take detours, God still _____ His promises.

04 — God's timing brings joy that man-made solutions never can.

When Isaac was born, Sarah's **laughter turned into testimony.**

vii. Sarah said, "God has made me _____."   (Genesis 21:6)

viii. Isaac's name means _____, because her sorrow turned into joy.

Let's Talk
About it

01. How do you think Sarah felt waiting so long for God's promise?

02. Ever laughed at something 'cause it felt impossible?

03. What's your response when it feels like God is delaying?

04. How does Sarah's story help you trust God with the things you're waiting for?

Your Trust Declaration

Write your own declaration of trust in God's timing. Be real. Release control and renew your faith.

"Christ lives in me. I am not feeble or forgotten. I am strong, and I am full of purpose. I exercise authority. I rule with love. I am a Daughter of the King, and I live like it."

Write yours:

_____

_____

_____

_____

_____

keep this somewhere you'll see it when you feel like giving up.

_____
Signed

_____
Date

Dig  Deeper

Pause for a sec. Time to hear what God says about you. Grab your Bible, a pen, and find a quiet spot. Ready? Let's go.

01. Look up each verse in your Bible (take your time).

02. Write the verse in your own words.

03. Ask: "What is God trying to tell ME?"

04. Write it down below!

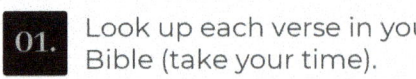

01. Genesis 18:14

Write the verse here:

What does it mean to you?

02. Psalm 27:14

Write the verse here:

What does it mean to you?

Dig *Deeper*

03. Romans 4:20–21

Write the verse here:

_____

_____

_____

What does it mean to you?

_____

_____

_____

04. Hebrews 11:11

Write the verse here:

_____

_____

_____

What does it mean to you?

_____

_____

_____

LET'S PRAY

Father,

Thank You for seeing every hope I carry. Even when my faith feels small, You remain faithful. Teach me to wait with joy instead of fear. Like Sarah, I want to laugh again; not from doubt, but from delight at what You've done. Help me trust You through every season. You are always on time. In Jesus' name, amen.

Take Action

Stop Doing

Answer

Do Less

Answer

Keep Doing

Answer

Do More

Answer

Start Doing

Answer

Affirmations
of the Week

01

I'm not forgotten. The One who called me won't quit on me.

02

I'm not hopeless. I'm waiting on God with expectation and joy.

03

I'm not defined by delays. I am defined by the promise of God.

04

I'm not ordinary. I carry a legacy of faith that will outlive me.

05

I'm not defined by doubt. I rejoice in His promise. If God said it, He will do it.

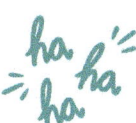

06

Not hopeless. Not sad. I will laugh. I will laugh with joy!

Say these out loud every day this week. This is who you are. This is how you lead.

SCAN ME

From God's Heart to *Yours!*
This page is just for you and God.

You've journeyed through six weeks of real women, real struggles, and real faith: from Mary's obedience to Hannah's surrender, and now with Sarah, it all points back to Him.

What did God show you along the way?

Did He remind you that His timing is perfect? Did He show you that His promises never expire? Did He grow your patience, your trust, or your hope?

Whatever He revealed to you, write it down here. This is your pilgrimage. From His heart... to yours.

My Notes from God this Week:

_____

_____

_____

_____

_____

_____

notes

"

Like Sarah, I want to laugh again; not
from doubt, but from delight at what
You've done. Help me trust You through
every season. You are always on time. In
Jesus' name, amen.

Maria Watkins

Yes Or No!

01 — Sarah gave Hagar to Abraham to try to "help" God's plan.

Yes ☐ No ☐

02 — Sarah never saw God's promise fulfilled.

Yes ☐ No ☐

03 — Sarah's story reminds us that God's promises don't expire.

Yes ☐ No ☐

04 — Sarah shows us that waiting is wasted time.

Yes ☐ No ☐

05 — Sarah's faith was always perfect, without mistakes.

Yes ☐ No ☐

06 — Sarah teaches us that even fragile faith can meet a faithful God.

Yes ☐ No ☐

THANK YOU!

FOR JOINING US

So, what's next?

Six weeks complete, and you're glowing with the strength of queens and prophets. Like Esther you've learned courage, like Hannah devotion, like Sarah trust, like Mary obedience, and like Deborah wisdom. But this is just the start. The King didn't crown you to hide your sparkle. God has called you to shine bright and share your light. Go forward, Rising Jewel!

Take the Challenge →

#Go4Ward

- ✓ Pick 4 younger girls—your friends, classmates, sisters, or even cousins.

- ✓ They each get a copy of this workbook.

- ✓ For the next 6 weeks, lead them through everything you've just learned.

- ✓ One chapter each week. One meet-up at a time.

You don't have to be perfect—just present, brave, and willing. Jesus didn't change the world alone. He built a team. And so will you. One courageous leader, four faithful sisters, one radiant mission. Ready to Go4Ward?

SCAN QR CODE →

#GO4WARD
PLEDGE

4 SISTERS. 1 MISSION.

My 'Yes' Starts now.

I've learned what it means to lead, follow God, and have purpose. Now I'm ready to PASS IT ON. I commit to being there for my 4 Sisters, week by week, word by word. 'll teach what I've learned. I'll pray for them. And I'll walk with them as we grow stronger together. We're not just friends; we're a movement. We Go 4Ward.

Signed: _____

Date: _____

My 4 Sisters:

✳ _____
✳ _____
✳ _____
✳ _____

Collect. Reflect. Share.

FREE DOWNLOADS:
Bible Character Gallery

We created beautiful digital images for every Bible heroine in this study: Esther, Mary, Deborah, Ruth, Hannah, and Sarah. And now, we're giving them to you for FREE. Why? Because God's Word should inspire you daily—and these visuals will help bring each story to life.

Scan the QR Code to unlock the full collection. Use them as wallpapers, study reminders, or share them with your sisters in faith. Go ahead, download the collection, and keep shining like the daughter of the King you are.

Scan to Download →

Tell the World What God Did! Your Voice Matters: Leave Us a Review on Google.

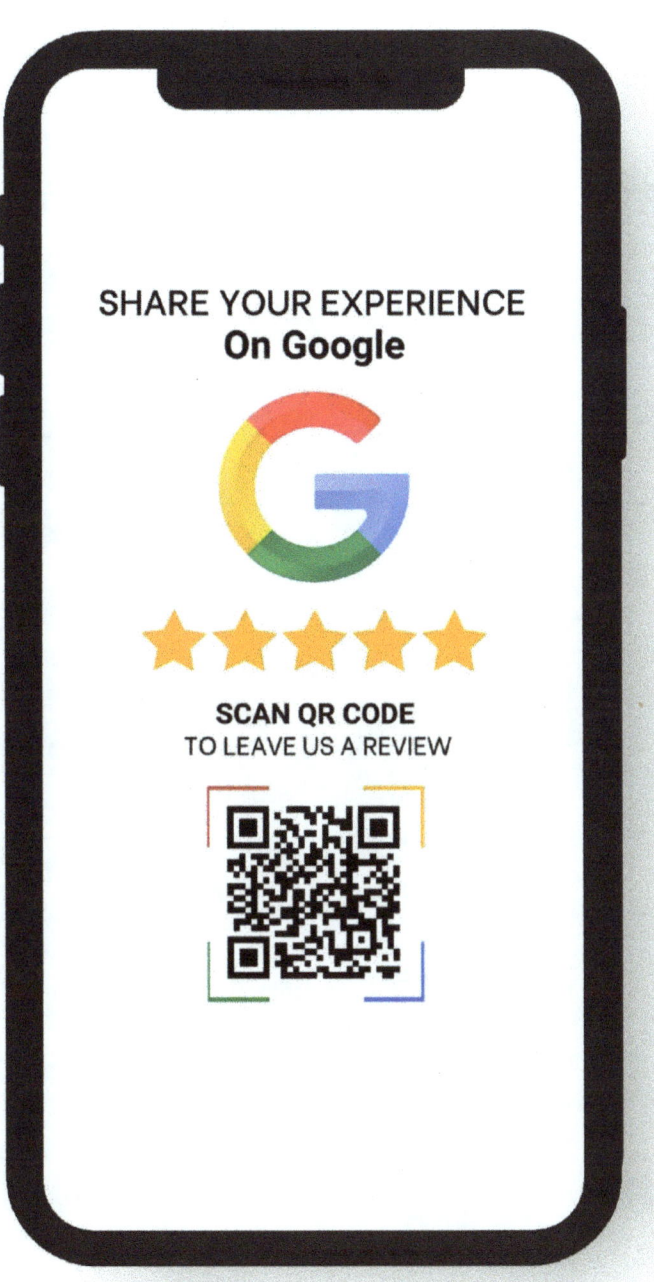

SHARE YOUR EXPERIENCE
On Google

★★★★★

SCAN QR CODE
TO LEAVE US A REVIEW

Did this workbook impact your life? Has your faith in God grown stronger through these six weeks?

Scan the QR code above to leave a review for Maria Watkins or Empowered Legacy Ministries on our official Google page. Your feedback encourages us, and helps others find the same hope and strength you've discovered! Speak life. Tell your story. Make folks aware that God is working!

About the Author

Maria Watkins is a woman marked by grace, grit, and God's guidance. Through Empowered Legacy Ministries, Maria serves men and women seeking more than surface success. Her heart is to mentor individuals (especially marketplace leaders and parents) through inner healing, spiritual warfare, and transformational identity work. She's especially gifted in discerning spiritual strongholds and equipping others to experience breakthrough and full restoration. Maria doesn't just preach success; she models holistic living: spirit, soul, and body aligned with purpose. Her ultimate desire is to see people become unrecognizable in the best way because of what God has done in them.

See next page for other books by:

Maria Watkins

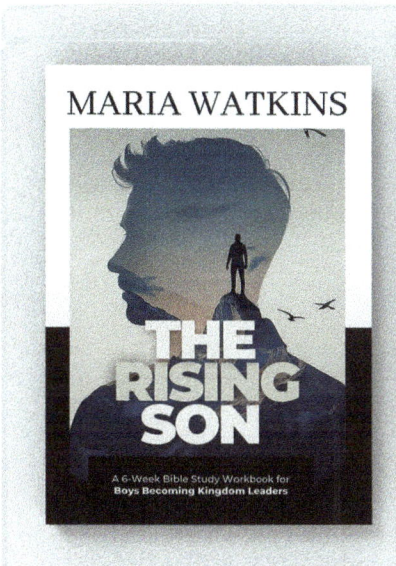

The Rising Son

Discover your purpose and walk boldly in faith with The Rising Son: A 6-Week Bible Study Workbook for Boys Becoming Kingdom Leaders. Made for teenagers, this interactive workbook shows how purity, identity, authority, and calling connect in a life dedicated to God.

SCAN TO BUY

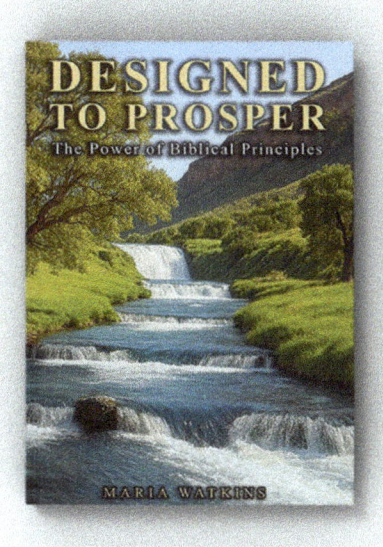

Designed to Prosper

Available in English & Spanish

If you're building a business, managing money, or dreaming of financial freedom, it's time to stop following the world's broken system and start applying the unshakable truths of the Kingdom. Designed to Prosper is your blue-print for mastering biblical finances and multiplying impact, God's way.

SCAN TO BUY

Hope Yet Again

Available in English & Spanish

This book was written with you in mind, with a heart full of love and a deep desire to remind you that God sees you, He hears your prayers, and He has not forgotten you. His promises are true, and His timing is perfect, even when it feels like all hope is lost.

SCAN TO BUY

Final Challenge is a Quiz

You've had 6 weeks of learning, growing, and stepping up. Now it's time to do your Final Challenge, and it's a QUIZ. The quiz covers everything you've learned from Esther, Mary, Deborah, Ruth, Hannah, and Sarah.

- Scan the QR code on this page to receive your Final Quiz. It's quick, fun, and helps you lock in what you've learned.

- Score 70% or higher, and we'll deliver a shareable PDF Certificate of Completion right to your inbox, because daughters of the King finish strong.

Congrats, Jewel

You did it! Six weeks of learning, growing, and discovering who you are in God. Now we need your feedback The following pages have short surveys just for you. Please take a few minutes to fill them out. Your answers really matter! Your feedback will make The Rising Jewel shine even brighter for the girls who come after you.

- Check each survey page for the QR code.
- Fill out the survey (just be real!).
- Snap a pic or screenshot of your answers.
- Scan the QR code to email it to Maria Watkins.

That's it! Quick. Simple. Powerful.

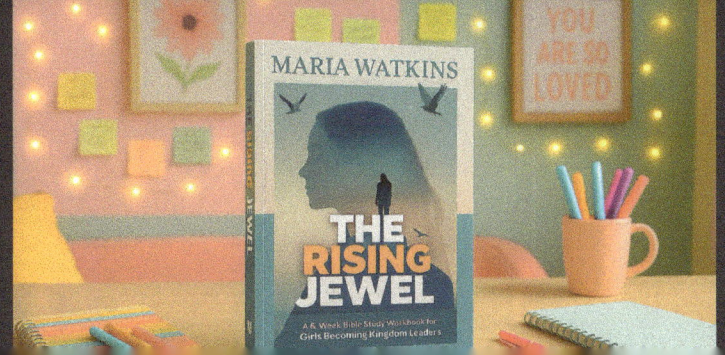

Survey.

Answer the Followng Questions On the scale of 1 to 10, one being very unlikely and ten being very likely.

01

How much did you enjoy this study?

01	02	03	04	05	06	07	08	09	10

02

How easy was it to follow along each week?

01	02	03	04	05	06	07	08	09	10

03

How much did the Bible characters inspire you?

01	02	03	04	05	06	07	08	09	10

04

How helpful were the affirmations and prayers?

01	02	03	04	05	06	07	08	09	10

05

How much did the workbook help you grow in faith?

01	02	03	04	05	06	07	08	09	10

01. The affirmations encouraged me each week.

Completely Disagree	Somewhat Agree	Neutral	Somewhat Agree	Completely Agree
01	02	03	04	05

02. I connected with the women of the Bible in a real way.

Completely Disagree	Somewhat Agree	Neutral	Somewhat Agree	Completely Agree
01	02	03	04	05

03. This workbook made me feel closer to God's purpose for me.

Completely Disagree	Somewhat Agree	Neutral	Somewhat Agree	Completely Agree
01	02	03	04	05

04. I would recommend The Rising Son to my friends.

Completely Disagree	Somewhat Agree	Neutral	Somewhat Agree	Completely Agree
01	02	03	04	05

SCAN ME

Finished your survey? Take a quick photo of this page, then scan the QR code. It will open an email where you can send your survey picture straight to Maria. She would love to hear from you!

Before You Go....

01. The best part of this study for me was...

_____

_____

_____

02. The Bible character I connected with most was...

_____

_____

_____

03. One way I will live differently after this study is...

_____

_____

_____

04. If I could share something about this workbook with a friend, I would say...

_____

_____